Animal World

Hens

Tessa Potter and Donna Bailey

STECK-VAUGHN
LIBRARY
A Division of Steck-Vaughn Company

There are many chickens
on this farm.
The female chickens are called hens.
They lay eggs we like to eat.

2

The male is called a rooster.
He has a big red comb on his head.

The hens run around the farm.
They look for food.

Hens have strong beaks and claws.
They peck and scratch up the ground.

The hens eat seeds, insects,
and green grass.
This hen is going to catch a worm.

These hens are having a dust bath.
They fluff up their feathers and
scratch up the dust.
They want to get rid of some fleas.
Fleas jump away from the dust.

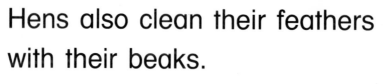

Hens also clean their feathers
with their beaks.
They nibble at the feathers.
They pull each one through their beaks.

8

One of the hens is moulting.
Hens moult every year.
Moulting is when old feathers come out
and new ones grow in.

9

At night the farmer puts the hens
in a chicken coop.
Foxes like to eat hens, but this fox
can't get inside the chicken coop.

The hens sleep inside a henhouse.
They sit on ledges in the henhouse.

Every day the farmer puts clean straw
on the floor of the henhouse.
He gives the hens fresh water to drink.

12

There are nest boxes in the henhouse.
The hens lay eggs in the nest boxes.

The farmer collects the eggs every day.
Look how many eggs he has!

The farmer checks the eggs and
sorts them into different sizes.

He packs the eggs into trays and boxes.
A truck takes the eggs to stores
where we buy them.

It is spring.
Some of these hens want to stay on
their nests all the time.
The farmer lets them keep their eggs.
The hens keep the eggs warm.

Look at this hen.

She has laid four eggs.

She stays on her nest all day.

Baby chicks grow in the eggs.
They will hatch out of the eggs
in three weeks.

The hen turns the eggs over with her beak and her feet.
Turning keeps the chicks inside the eggs from sticking to the shells.

It is time for the chicks
to come out of the eggs.
A baby chick breaks the shell
with its beak.

The chick pushes out of the shell.
It is wet and tired.

22

These chicks are one day old.
Their feathers are dry and fluffy.

The hen takes care of her chicks.
She teaches them to look for food.

This farmer keeps hens on his farm.

The hens live in cages in a shed.

The hens can't run around.

The farmer gives the hens food to eat.
He gives them water to drink.
The hens lay eggs for the farmer.
Their eggs roll outside the cages.

The farmer collects the eggs
from the shed.
He puts them into a big machine that
sorts the eggs into different sizes.

People pack the eggs into cartons.
The farmer sells the cartons of eggs.
We can buy them
in the grocery store.

The hens in these cages have been mated
with a rooster.
Now baby chicks will grow in the eggs
the hens lay.

The hens do not take care of their eggs.
The farmer takes the eggs away.
Now the hens can lay more eggs
for the farmer.

The farmer puts the eggs into warm trays.
The baby chicks hatch out in the trays.
A special light keeps the chicks warm.

The farmer sells the chicks
to other farmers.
Some of the chicks are lucky.
They will live in a farmyard with
other hens and a rooster.

Index

Reading Consultant: Diana Bentley
Editorial Consultant: Donna Bailey
Supervising Editor: Kathleen Fitzgibbon

Illustrated by Gill Tomblin
Picture research by Suzanne Williams
Designed by Richard Garratt Design

Photographs
Cover: Peter Greenland
Farmers Weekly: 25, 27, 28 and 32
Frank Lane Picture Agency: 10 (David Grewcock)
Peter Greenland: 1, 2, 3, 4, 5, 6, 7, 11, 12, 13, 14, 15, 16, 17, 18 and 19
NHPA: 21, 22 and 23 (G. I. Bernard), 26 (David Woodfall)
OSF Picture Library: 29 (Animals Animals)
ZEFA: 24

Library of Congress Cataloging-in-Publication Data: Potter, Tessa. Hens/Tessa Potter and Donna Bailey; [illustrated by Gill Tomblin]. p. cm.—(Animal world) SUMMARY: Discusses the life of hens that produce eggs to be sold. Portrays hens that run freely about the farm and those that never leave their cages. ISBN 0-8114-2627-0 1. Chickens—Juvenile literature. [1. Chickens.] I. Bailey, Donna. II. Tomblin, Gill, ill. III. Title. IV. Series: Animal world (Austin, Tex.) SF 487.5.P67 1990 636.5'142—dc20 89-22020 CIP AC